A
Glimpse of
DARTMOOR

PRISON

Trevor James

"Liberty is more to be desired than fetters of gold"
Michael Davitt, 1885 (former Dartmoor prisoner)

**Peninsula
Press**

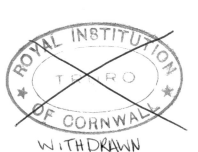

──────── **ACKNOWLEDGEMENTS** ────────

The author expresses his gratitude to everyone who helped with this book. Special thanks are due to the Governor of Dartmoor Prison Mr John Lawrence, and his predecessor Mr John Powls, both of whom kindly extended facilities and assisted in other ways. I appreciate the contribution of material and photographs from friends and acquaintances, some perfect strangers, and various members of staff at Dartmoor, in particular Prison Officer Mike Chamberlain who was more than generous with information and advice, and Mr John Conduit, Head of Works, for his kind help.

This work is respectfully dedicated in fond remembrance of my grandparents the late Mr and Mrs Charlie Doidge of Tavistock.

Published by Peninsula Press Ltd
P.O. Box 31
Newton Abbot
Devon TQ12 5XH

Tel 01803 875875

© Trevor James 1995

Printed in England by Exe Print, Exeter, Devon.

ISBN I 872640 17 6

A GLIMPSE OF DARTMOOR · PRISON ·

Contents

Dartmoor Prison 1994

"Consider the height of the prison blocks and imagine abseiling down on a black winter night"
(Photo by courtesy of Mr B. Jones)

FOREWORD

I am delighted, as the 37th Governor of Dartmoor Prison, to introduce this book.

Dartmoor has been a significant landmark on the Moors for nearly 200 years; its reputation as a "hard" prison known to all.

In fact, it has changed dramatically over the years — not just physically but in ethos. It has a training regime which is second to none; security and rehabilitation are its watchwords.

I hope you will enjoy this book, which aims to give a taste of this old prison as we end the 20th century.

John Lawrence, Governor, September 1994

Introduction

Dartmoor Prison is situated over 1,400 feet above sea level on one of the bleakest parts of southern England. It is exposed to savage winters. The gales sometimes bring snow which drifts several feet deep and the intense cold and freezing fogs are legendary. In summer there are often days of thick wet mist which tend to depress the town dweller.

The remoteness and harsh climate have, since the Napoleonic Wars, given the place a bad reputation. During the Victorian convict era it was feared by criminals and hated by prison warders, many of whom were, in later years, drafted here for compulsory service from establishments all over Britain. It was the only way to maintain staffing levels. Some of the houses they occupied can still be seen. Most officers nowadays commute from Plymouth and Tavistock where their families have access to the towns' facilities. For the inmates, visits by families and friends are a problem as it is not an easy place to get to and many of them come from as far away as Liverpool, which entails an overnight stay. Not everyone can manage this, for a variety of reasons, so for many, the weekly visiting "ration" of two hours is saved and squandered on one day visit a month.

Princetown developed in the prison's shadow and the village has seen hectic times. The French prisoners of war, the Americans captured in the war of 1812, the Militia troops who guarded them, and later, criminal classes of every kind trod the path to the prison gate. The car thief and the murderer; child abusers and confidence tricksters; men from the slums and public schoolboys; bank robbers and evil monsters — the prison staff have seen them all. The full Dartmoor story could never be told, it is too rich in variety and unbelievable truths, and one's imagination would not match such a tale. Here though, is an outline to stimulate your thoughts, perhaps satisfy your curiosity, and give you some idea of "life inside".

The Beginning

The prison owes its existence to Sir Thomas Tyrwhitt, Lord Warden of the Stannaries, and personal friend of the Prince of Wales (future Prince Regent and King George IV) after whom Prince Town (as it was first known) was named. As the Sovereign's eldest son and Duke of Cornwall, he owned the Forest of Dartmoor, as indeed HRH Prince Charles does today, and leased the land to several developers, including Sir Thomas, whose dream it was to turn Prince Town into an agricultural centre and bring prosperity to what was then a wilderness. He built Tor Royal as a country house and estate from where he could direct operations and entertain his friends. The house remains standing today and the estate is still being farmed.

Success however came about by means other than by tilling the moorland soil. In 1803 Britain resumed war with France and was soon inundated with thousands of prisoners who quickly filled the old war prisons and compelled the government to make use once again of the terrible hulks – dismasted shells of old men o' war. Over forty of these floating prisons were anchored off shore at Chatham, Portsmouth and Plymouth. Men were confined below decks in unsanitary, overcrowded conditions with little exercise, breathing stale air when the hatches were closed for the night.

Consequently the death rate rose to an unacceptably high level, mostly from chest diseases and typhus. The cost of maintenance was high. At Plymouth the hulks were thought to be a threat to the important naval base and arsenal, should a mass escape occur. Such attempts had been made and the authorities determined to build a new war prison at a safe distance. Sir Thomas seized his chance, using his position and Royal connections to influence the choice of site – the spot where the prison stands today. His life and work, the history of Princetown, and the story of the prison are forever entwined.

Dartmoor Depot, as it was first called, was built between 1806 and 1809 under the personal supervision of the architect, Mr Daniel Alexander, one of the most experienced men of that time. Timber was scarce and expensive so, although it was intended to be a temporary place of confinement, our most famous prison was built of moorstone (surface stone which you can see scattered all over Dartmoor) supplemented by granite from the nearby quarries. The stone was broken up on the spot by gangs of workmen and dressed by stonemasons, mainly Cornishmen. The location was ideal in some respects – it was secure, there was plenty of stone, and ample water was available from the River Walkham via the 4 mile long Prison Leat, which continues to supply water for sanitary purposes and for the farm animals to drink. The final cost of the prison was £135,000, almost double the estimate, due to foul weather and demands for higher wages by the masons, causing delays.

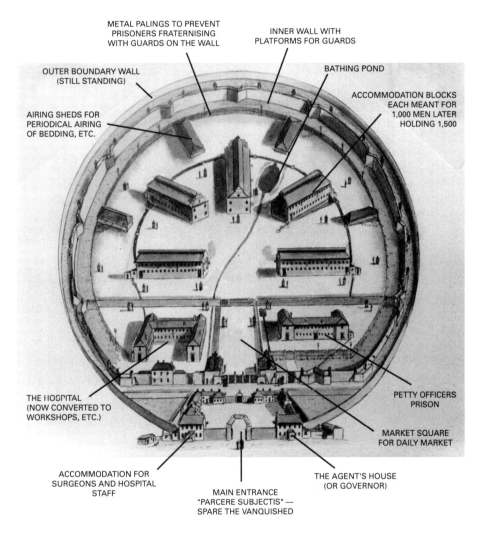

METAL PALINGS TO PREVENT PRISONERS FRATERNISING WITH GUARDS ON THE WALL

INNER WALL WITH PLATFORMS FOR GUARDS

OUTER BOUNDARY WALL (STILL STANDING)

BATHING POND

ACCOMMODATION BLOCKS EACH MEANT FOR 1,000 MEN LATER HOLDING 1,500

AIRING SHEDS FOR PERIODICAL AIRING OF BEDDING, ETC.

THE HOSPITAL (NOW CONVERTED TO WORKSHOPS, ETC.)

PETTY OFFICERS PRISON

MARKET SQUARE FOR DAILY MARKET

ACCOMMODATION FOR SURGEONS AND HOSPITAL STAFF

MAIN ENTRANCE "PARCERE SUBJECTIS" — SPARE THE VANQUISHED

THE AGENT'S HOUSE (OR GOVERNOR)

(From a painting by Paul Deacon of an old manuscript)

French and American POWs

The Depot was designed to hold 5,000 men but by the end of 1813 there were over 9,000 prisoners including the newly-arrived Americans from the war of 1812. There were originally five three-storey blocks, each meant to hold 1,000 men. Over 1,500 were later crammed in and two extra blocks were built by the prisoners. The establishment was run on naval lines under the command of "Agents" invariably Post Captains from the Royal Navy. The prisoners slept in hammocks (no hardship to the majority, who were seamen) and on the concrete floors in dormitories without heating and unglazed 2 foot square windows. It was the heat generated by their closely packed bodies which kept them alive one severe winter when water froze solid in buckets and snow drifts reached the top of the boundary wall, the same wall you see today. They lived on the standard RN rations of that period:

Ration per day per man: $1\frac{1}{2}$ lb bread, $\frac{1}{2}$ lb beef, $\frac{1}{2}$ lb greens or turnips, $\frac{1}{4}$ oz onions, $\frac{1}{3}$ oz salt.

The cooks, who were recruited from the prisoners, served up the ration in the form of a broth with one 9lb loaf for each "mess" of six men. Twice a week 1lb fish was substituted for the beef and 1lb potatoes were issued in lieu of greens or turnips.

French POWs marching to Dartmoor Prison. (From a painting hanging in the prison hospital, by a former inmate)

A old photograph of one of the original French prisons before conversion to a modern block.

The "Market Square" looking toward Main Gate.
(From a painting hanging in the prison hospital by a former inmate)

Gambling was the main recreation. Many men lost all they had including bedding, clothes and sometimes their rations on "one throw of pitch and toss". As a result several of them died of malnutrition and exposure. Diseases took their toll from the start and in that first winter of 1809 there was a measles epidemic which killed 465 French inmates In total over 1,200 died during the years of captivity. The Americans lost 267 of their number mostly during an outbreak of smallpox in the winter of 1814, by which time the French war had ended and the prisoners had gone home. Napoleon was exiled to the Mediterranean island of Elba but in April 1815 he escaped and fought to win back all he had lost, only to be defeated at Waterloo — the "Hundred Days". Many French prisoners found themselves back at Dartmoor a second time just as the Americans were leaving.

American mass grave and memorial. The French had a separate plot with an identical obelisk.

The dead were buried on the open moor outside the prison walls. By 1866 the shallow graves had become exposed through weathering and the attentions of wild animals. Human bones littered the area. Under the direction of the prison Governor, Captain W. Stopford, they were collected, divided and interred in two separate cemeteries — one French, one

The Victorian era. Prison warders outside the main entrance. (Photo by courtesy of R.G.Sandford)

American. These are situated under the trees at the rear of the prison. Two obelisks surmount the mass graves, each bearing the inscription Dulce et Decorum est pro Patria Mori (it is sweet and honourable to die for one's country).

The huge stone arch straddling the main entrance is aptly inscribed PARCERE SUBJECTIS (Spare the Vanquished). The quotation is by the poet Virgil in an entreaty to the Romans to spare their defeated enemies instead of killing them as was the custom in ancient times.

Princetown grew with the prison. A barracks was built to house the Militia guards. Every kind of trade was to be seen and the streets teemed with activity. There was a slaughterhouse, two bakeries and blacksmiths, coopers, millers and brewers, to name but a few. Today's High Moorland Visitor Centre was once the officers' quarters, afterwards converted to a hotel. At first there were 500 officers and men, rising to 1,200 as the number of prisoners increased. The town flourished whilst the prisoners suffered.

Most officer POWs lived in nearby towns on parole as free men providing they gave their word of honour not to try and escape. Despite this several hundred did abscond, a number of generals among them. Those who were caught breaking their parole conditions or who refused parole were confined in a separate walled-in prison known as *Le Petit Cautionnement* (Little Parole); the British called it the "Petty Officers' Prison", and it is now a listed building. Officers on parole lived with local families or were allocated houses by the "Agents" appointed to supervise them. They were paid two shillings (10p) a week subsistence but many had private funds from France or supplemented their income by teaching languages, music or painting. There were clever artisans among the rank and file. They built Princetown Church, afterwards completed by the Americans, the only church in England built by prisoners of war. Other prisoners

Church of St Michael and all Angels, Princetown, built by French and American POWs. (The church is now closed)

1st Devon Militia: officer and private, review order, 1812.

made exquisite artefacts out of bone and odd bits of wood, including beautiful models of buildings and ships in complete detail. These were exchanged or sold at the daily market held within the prison for poultry, tobacco and fresh vegetables brought by the country folk and pedlars from Plymouth. Several Frenchmen on parole married local women and remained in England after the war. Some are buried in local churchyards and their names in the parish records remind us of a unique period in the prison's history.

Painted figures carved from the vertebrae of an ox by French POWs. (Courtesy of Launceston Museum)

Escapers were either shot or bayonetted in the attempt. Those who were recaptured were punished by confinement in the "Black Hole", a 20 foot square stone cell without bedding or straw, and on a restricted diet. Several French and Americans escaped by bribing the soldiers to help them. The garrison was changed

Uncompleted Man o' War made by French POWs from meat bones. (Courtesy of Launceston Museum)

every three months to help prevent this. The most spectacular escape, and a well documented one, was that of a French officer, Louis Vanhille, who mingled with the market people and departed with them in disguise. After several months "on the run" and with ample funds provided by English friends he got as far as Jamaica, hoping to get home via America, but was detected and sent back to finish the war aboard the hulks.

The Americans were unruly, boisterous, rebellious prisoners, defiant to the end. They dug tunnels in daring escape attempts, taunted their guards and quarrelled with the French. On 6 April 1815 whilst awaiting repatriation after their war had ended, their wilful behaviour provoked the guards into firing on them. Nine men were killed and over thirty wounded. The "Princetown Massacre" was a black day in British military history.

The Prisoners go Home

The "Yankees" went home at last followed by the French. By February 1816 the prison was deserted and Princetown fell into decay, eventually becoming a ghost town. Sir Thomas Tyrwhitt was back where he started. In a valiant effort to retrieve the situation he helped form a company which built a horse-drawn railway from Plymouth. It was opened in 1823 with the intention of exporting granite and farm products from the moor, and importing lime and timber, as well as sea sand for manure. It failed to attract the interest he hoped for and he died a poor man in 1833. A memorial tablet in the church expresses an appreciation of his efforts.

It was to be the prison which restored Princetown's fortunes again. The British Patent Naphtha Company leased it in 1846 for the production of gas and oils. The scars can still be seen on the left hand side of the Rundlestone-Two Bridges road where peat was extracted by the ton and transported across the road and over the prison walls by a tramway. However the yield and quality of the gas was poor and the company went into liquidation shortly afterwards.

A New Beginning

At this point in our history the colonies were refusing to accept Britain's convicted criminals and except for Western Australia, transportation ceased after 1853. Britain now had to deal with her own convicts. Portsmouth and Portland were opened as working establishments where work similar to that done by transported men could be simulated. Dartmoor was selected for the same role but for sick and disabled convicts who it was thought would benefit from the country air. In September 1850 a band of convict artisans converted one of the old blocks for penal use, constructing individual cells of corrugated iron back to back down the centre of the dormitories. The guards were to patrol between them and the walls. About 200 prisoners arrived in November under the charge of Captain Gambier, the first Governor. Men of the Royal Lancaster Regiment were the first of several army units to guard them. Most of those early inmates were men with chest complaints; others had deformities — crooked spines and so on — and there were men with wooden legs. Dartmoor was really a kind of sanatorium where sick prisoners from the convict hulks still in use (the *Garth* and *Stirling Castle* at Gosport, and the *Warrior* and *Defence* at Woolwich) and the "hospital" prison at Woking were sent. Abuse of the system led in time to the most vicious and troublesome men being transferred to Dartmoor and it became a dumping ground for undesirables, thus acquiring its reputation as a tough prison, a charge still made today and for the same (now untrue) reasons. It was tough in other ways. Many of the warders were hard men recruited from the mining communities. The prisoners' work was back-breaking toil in the quarries and on the land. Men worked under armed guard breaking stones for roadmaking and repairs to prison buildings. One convict recounted how they were issued with cloth bags to cover their hands in winter to prevent frostbite and chilblains. In the 1870s Michael Davitt, a one-armed Fenian sympathiser, broke stones and was expected to perform as well as the other men. He ended up in the prison hospital unable to fend for himself because of the blistering to his one hand. He afterwards visited Dartmoor with a party of MPs and signed his name in the Visitor's Book with his old convict number.

One of the clauses in the new ninety-nine year Duchy lease stipulated the prison lands should be cultivated (25 acres per year) and this was done by gangs of convicts who dug the virgin moor by hand in line abreast. Over a ten-year period it was calculated that 200 men would dig and lay out the fields and watercourses which are visible today. One man wrote: "The labour was hard for brutish half starved men, weakened by long confinement, standing in water up to two foot deep and spading peat." Boulders were removed by dragging them away on wooden sleds. Manure from the prison cesspit was carted to site and interred with farmyard manure and lime. The now fertile soil produced excellent crops of potatoes, turnips, and some cereal. Probably the worst job was in the bone shed next to the prison cesspit where meat bones were reduced to powder by a steam driven crushing machine, and later by hand in a building a mere 20 feet by 10 feet. In choking dust and summer heat it must have been killing work.

The Victorian Convicts

By 1857 there were 1,158 convicts in the prison. Their uniform was described thus "...each man was dressed in a short loose jacket and vest, and baggy knickerbockers of drab tweed with black stripes, each one and a half inches broad. The lower part of their legs were encased in worsted stockings with bright red rings round them and a bright red and grey cap..." Over the whole of the clothing was stamped the broad arrow or "crow's foot" and their boots had nails in the shape of an arrow hammered in the soles which left an imprint wherever they trod. (The "arrow" logo originated in the Board of Ordnance who supplied the prison and army equipment which was marked thus to discourage hard-up soldiers from selling it.) The military guards were finally replaced by a civil guard (mostly ex-

The Victorian prison: a work party leaving the main entrance.

The Victorian prison: convicts shackled to a work cart – once a common sight in Princetown.

army pensioners) whose duties were to provide armed escorts for the working parties. In the 1870s visitors of both sexes were regularly shown around the prison and when the men went to their work sightseers congregated at the gate. What did those early visitors find? The most profound impact must have been the total silence. The Silent Rule, an American idea, was designed to prevent young convicts from being corrupted by the "old lags", and was strictly enforced. It was combined with solitary confinement at night. Silence meant no talking, whispering, nodding of heads or looking at anyone. In the tailoring shop a prisoner who required more thread for example held up his hand and when noticed by the warder in charge asked "More thread please sir?" A curt nod and he would turn to his companion to receive it. Even the warders were penalised by black marks on their conduct sheets if they broke silence on duty.

The corrugated iron cells were sought after as being the warmest and driest. Most of the stone-built ones had water trickling down the walls (granite being porous) and the resulting pools had to be mopped up several times a day. Initially hammocks were provided though later the bedding consisted of wooden planks with two blankets and a coir pillow. Candlelight was eventually supplanted by gas, produced in the prison gasworks from peat and then coal.

Food was little better than that enjoyed by the Napoleonic prisoners. A typical day's menu was: Breakfast: Gruel and bread. Dinner: Boiled meat, suet pudding or soup, potatoes and bread. Supper: Cocoa and bread. The men were always hungry and it is on record that some were seen to eat candles, dubbin, and grass. They rose at 5am and were locked up for the night at 7.45pm. Lights Out was at 7.55pm and mighty glad they must have been for the oblivion that comes with sleep.

By the turn of the century the following occupations were employed: farming and cattle breeding, with pigs, cattle, sheep and horses all taking prizes at local shows. Shoemaking: boots for the Prison Service and the Metropolitan Police made by convicts under supervision. Tailoring: uniforms were made as above. Stone cutting and quarrying: there were fatalities and some men were disfigured for life in accidents. Twine shop: for the manufacture of twine. Stonemasonry: stone was dressed and used for building and repairs at Dartmoor, Exeter Prison, and some London prisons. Carpentry: there was a workshop with a steam driven circular saw. Blacksmith's shop: wrought ironwork formerly done under contract by the Princetown "smithy" was performed under supervision by the inmates. This continues today with bars and gates manufactured on site by the men they are designed to contain.

The prison was a little township and practically self-supporting. For many years the farm had the services of the "Dartmoor Shepherd", a Welshman called David Davies who was a compulsive offertory box robber. He was in and out of Dartmoor regularly

Dartmoor Prison work party setting off during the Victorian era. (Photo by courtesy of R.G.Sandford)

The Victorian Prison: guard at inner gateway, and old administration block in the background; the area between the outer and inner gateway is now totally enclosed.

and came to know his flock so well he called individual sheep to him by name. Prime Minister David Lloyd George witnessed the phenomenon on a visit and conversed with him in Welsh.

Under the leadership of Sir Joshua Jebb, one of the first Chairmen of the Directors of Prisons and a deeply religious man, an attempt was made to rehabilitate convicted men by a mixture of kindness and repression. The latter was nine months' solitary confinement picking oakum (tarred rope) in a bare cell with only the Bible and a Prayer Book to read for all long term prisoners, before they were moved to where they would serve their sentences. This was to "break them in" to the rigours of prison life and enable them to reflect on their wrongdoings. Good behaviour was rewarded by allowing them to grow their hair and beards (normally cut as short as the scissors would go) and extra letter writing. Food was so plentiful that Dartmoor families sent their children daily to the prison to collect any bread that was left over. They came to rely on this and were hard hit when Sir Joshua died in 1863.

The convicts were hard hit too for the system changed under Sir Edmund Du Cane who, after a short interval, replaced him. The discipline became severe and work was designed as a punishment to the degree that should a man get some satisfaction from a job well done it was thought it would detract from its purpose! The new regime was accompanied by an increase in assaults on prison staff. More than one warder was almost killed by attacks with spades and other implements at Dartmoor. The wrath of the prison system then descended on the culprits. Minor offences earned solitary confinement on the famous weight reducing "jockey" diet – three days' bread and water. Other offences were punished by loss of privileges such as letter writing. The ultimate deterrent was the "cat o' nine tails" (a whip with nine leather lashes or "tails") and the birch rod, reserved for mutinous behaviour or for striking an officer. The cat o' nine tails was rendered more humane during the present century by the provision of a canvas jacket to protect the kidneys, with a square cut out of the back, and an issue of brandy afterwards. The fixtures for securing the "Triangle" to which the victim was strapped can still be seen in the punishment block at Dartmoor. This hideous act was carried out under the supervision of the Medical Officer and it was admitted by many who witnessed it to be a degrading experience. Convicts were paraded to witness such punishments long after they had been abolished in the army and navy. The reaction of the victims ranged from being totally broken in mind and spirit, to defiance. One man is recorded as taking his "dozen" without a murmur, then turning to his tormentors and saying, "Right! Now I'll fight the best man amongst you!" It was the birch though that was hated and feared the most, probably on account of the indignity imposed whilst administering it.

Escapes

Dartmoor, like every prison, has its repertoire of escape stories, many of them dramatised because of the surrounding moors. A popular misconception is of fugitives being pursued over the bogs in swirling mist by officers with bloodhounds. The prison never kept bloodhounds though one was borrowed once from a local resident and the escaper was caught on the outskirts of Plymouth. Until recent years Dartmoor had mounted warders who were acquainted with the moor and had alloted areas to cover in the event of an escape. The alarm was once raised by a gunshot, then a warning bell took its place and this in turn gave way to a siren. With the advent of radio communication they are all now obsolete.

Escapes usually occurred in bad weather and almost always from outside working parties whose armed guards used to open fire (aiming at the legs) only after shouting three warnings. Some men were killed. Those who made it out of sight had the moor to contend with. Many a man has gladly surrendered having got hopelessly lost and frozen with cold and wet. A former Governor, Mr Basil Thomson, joined one search on horseback and came across the escaped man "shivering and irresolute, anxious only to be recaptured. In fact when he saw me," wrote the Governor, "instead of running away he approached me and scrambled over a wall to my side. I have never seen so miserable an object."

In February 1853 a man called Brown escaped in a blizzard. A couple of days later a farmer found him collapsed in his farmyard and took him in. The police came and removed him to Tavistock Hospital. The prison Governor, on being informed, said he would send officers to bring him back. "I'm afraid that won't be possible for a while, Sir," was the reply. "You see, he's had his toes amputated. Frostbite, Sir." It was surely a bitter price to pay for so short a spell of freedom.

In 1860 a number of young offenders were transferred from Parkhurst. Two of them, both under 12 years old, scaled the wall with the help of an older convict and were never seen again. Every trick you have ever heard of has been tried by would-be escapers at Dartmoor – the proverbial tying together of bedsheets and blankets to use as ropes – manufacturing dummy keys – one was made of meat bones, another of wood – tearing up floors, chipping away at the masonry and prising stones from the walls. Consider the height of the prison blocks and imagine abseiling down the outside on a black winter night using an improvised rope as just described and you cannot but join in the grudging admiration the "screws" had for the bravery of those men. "Rubberbones Webb" who got out by crawling through the warm air ducts, and Frank

Mitchell the "Mad Axeman", who vanished from an outside working party and was never found, are the legendary names remembered by the older hands, but the most daring escape in modern times took place on 24 June 1963, when a group of prisoners led by a man named Jennings stole a tanker that had just completed an oil delivery to the boiler house. They drove it around the perimeter wall and reversed on to the grass football pitch opposite thick double wooden doors leading to the outside farm area. The driver "gunned" the accelerator and the truck burst through the doors to freedom. The doors have since been removed and the aperture walled up, but the "Jennings Taxi" legend lives on.

"Jennings Taxi": the fugitives, three in number, were all caught hiding in woods near Warren House.

The moors and the border country can be dangerous and some escapers never got off them. The author recalls several instances of serious injury and death of men on the run. They have fallen into quarries and rivers, and one was drowned in Burrator Reservoir. There is a lighter side though. Mr Ron Chudley, a retired *Western Morning News* reporter relates an incident from his young days when an escaped convict story always made good copy. He was sent to Dartmoor to report on a breakout when, passing through Merrivale, he was overwhelmed by a feeling that the fugitive was hiding in the quarry there. He spent a long time standing in the gateway looking for signs of movement. Finally, he decided to go on to the prison and await developments.

He was there with several others when the recaptured man was brought in. Looking at Ron the convict yelled "I know you!" Everybody stared. "You're the bloke wot was looking straight at me in the quarry!" he laughed.

Only one man is known to have broken into Dartmoor. Joe Denny was found skulking in the yards on 17 August 1890. He had recently been released from the prison but, harbouring a hatred for one of the warders, had come back seeking revenge. He intended setting fire to the place. He was up before Tavistock magistrates the next day on a charge of burglary! He died later in prison.

Boy convicts at Portsmouth Prison 1898. Young boy convicts such as these were transferred to Dartmoor from Parkhurst (Isle of Wight) in 1860. (Photo by courtesy of Hampshire County Council)

The 20th Century Prison

Up until 1902 convicts who died in the prison were buried in a separate plot in Princetown churchyard in unmarked graves. After that date the authorities put small granite headstones over them inscribed with the date of death and the deceased's initials. Today you can see the rows of stones to the right and rear of the church.

The large granite cross close to the tower was made and erected by convict labour in 1912 as a memorial to all those prisoners who lie in unmarked graves. Relatives always had the right to place headstones over their loved ones and the only two ever erected by them can be seen in isolation from the rest. One is to a convict, with the inscription "L.D.C. who died February 2nd 1877. My Jesu Mercy". The second one simply says "R.G.P. 9-7-'46" and is to a Borstal boy.

Princetown churchyard: the sad bleak rows of headstones bearing convicts' initials and date of death.

Princetown churchyard: memorial cross for convicts buried in unmarked graves.

The prison gasworks provided light and heat. Today modern oil fired boilers provide heat, and electric lighting brightens the interior. The large double prison block centre left was demolished in the 1950s.

World War I saw the prison emptied of convicts in 1917 and their places taken by 1,000 conscientious objectors. The men were ostracised generally but the prison staff seem to have treated them fairly. They were put to work on the roads and a section of road leading past Tor Royal towards Batchelors Hall is known to this day as "Conchie Road". The prison, in common with the civilian population, had to trim its rations and one new regulation stipulated that "Jam Roly-Polies should be made without syrup or jam"!

Conditions slowly improved after the war, but new convicts taking a "trip over the alps" as the convicts used to say, still had to wait four years on good behaviour before they had the privilege of smoking and reading newspapers. Today it is every prisoner's right to have whatever he asks to be sent in from the newsagents, providing he can pay for it, and there is no ban on smoking. The Silent Rule was finally abolished but the "Fool's Parade", the single file circular walk which passed for exercise, continued. Now the prison has a beautifully equipped gymnasium and football, among other sports, is actively encouraged.

Mutiny

When men are driven to the limit of endurance, mental or physical, for reasons real or imagined, they rebel. Many a ship's captain and army commander have had to contend with it. In prison, with hundreds of frustrated men in close confinement, the "screws" man the front line among their charges, any one of whom could, under certain conditions, set off an explosion of violence.

Such was the famous mutiny of January 1932 when nearly 200 prisoners went on the rampage, smashing up everything in their path including the chapel and the officers' mess, and setting fire to the entire administration block and the Governor's office, which were completely gutted. The Governor and a Home Office official on a visit barely escaped with their lives. Police and army units from Plymouth were called upon to help quell the disturbance. Several prisoners and staff were hurt, some seriously, before normality was restored. The late Mr W. Halfyard of Princetown told me how, as a young man, he had spent the day watching the proceedings from a vantage point in a tree overlooking the prison yards. "The ringleaders were afterwards tried in the old Town Hall" (since demolished) he said, adding, "It was the prison wall that contained the mutiny. The prisoners had possession of the entire prison and would undoubtedly have broken free."

Several prisoners were rewarded for defending warders from attack by having their sentences reduced; others were rewarded by up to 12 years' extra imprisonment for the part they played.

The more recent riots of April 1990 have attracted wide publicity and speculation, some of it ill-informed. In the end it is the quality and attitude of the staff which is vital in solving the day to day problems that arise — it is the accumulation of these which often leads to confrontation.

Princetown Town Hall, 17th March 1932 during the trial of prisoners following the Mutiny.

Front of offices from right of main drive, gutted during the Mutiny.

World War II

In 1939 there were over 300 prisoners at Dartmoor, some of whom were IRA men. 20th century terrorist attacks are nothing new — the IRA were active in Britain as long ago as the 1860s when their forerunners, the Fenians, raised mayhem here. In August 1939 there was a serious attack on the Dartmoor IRA convicts by other inmates following an explosion in Coventry which killed six people. The Governor's journal for 21 August notes: ".. certain prisoners of the IRA made injudicious remarks concerning this incident. Of the eleven IRA prisoners on parade all were assaulted." There was further trouble when they incited other men to reject their dinners and refuse work.

The journal records the outbreak of war on 3 September 1939. The next day the Governor received 49 "applicants" most of whom were petitioning to join the armed forces. The following story was related to the author by a retired army colonel: "At the beginning of the war I had in my unit a man named 'Ruby' Sparks who was one of the instigators of the 1932 mutiny at Dartmoor. [Charles John Sparks got four years added to his sentence for inciting others to arson. He also saved a warder from serious injury.] I found he was first class material and we turned him into a very good soldier." "Did he survive the war?" The Colonel sighed ruefully. "Well, I'm afraid he got 'nicked' for black market dealing in identity cards and went back to prison," he replied. "That was a pity because I'm quite certain he was innocent on this occasion." During the course of two world wars convict volunteers won at least one VC and many other decorations for valour.

A number of "glasshouse" military prisoners came to Dartmoor from Chelmsford in 1939. The Governor was an ex-army man and was not impressed by them. His orders were that the slightest insubordination "must be dealt with very firmly". He was put to the test several months later when a number of men in each hall refused to go to the cells. "I ordered large staves to be issued to officers and I went to the halls," he wrote. "After some demur they went to the cells." The duration of "demur" must have been lively but such a course of action would be unthinkable today.

The prison ran like clockwork under an iron hand. Assaults on staff were relentlessly followed a week or so later by corporal punishment, mainly with the "cat". These years were anxious ones for everyone, what with air raid warnings, gas mask drills, and fire drills. Light relief took the form of amateur dramatics by visiting societies, gramophone concerts and on 10 March 1940 the first cinematograph (film) show. On one occasion the famous Geraldo and his band performed and the Governor's comments speak volumes about Dartmoor weather: "I allowed this concert on a Saturday afternoon... during the last 62 days we have had 54 days of almost continual rain with the result everyone is rather depressed." This was written on 12 August.

On 15 November 1945 the first 40 Borstal boys were admitted. They were young men aged between 16 and 21, mostly vicious thugs who had been convicted of crimes the likes of which are so prevalent in Britain now. The number of breaches of discipline and escapes rose when they arrived.

Modern Times

Dartmoor is changing fast. New ideas and a £27 million facelift are transforming a gloomy complex into cleaner, brighter, more hygienic quarters. The old communal bath-houses where prisoners bathed once a week have closed. Now there are showers in every prison block and no restrictions on their use. "Slopping out" is coming to an end – a programme of refurbishment is under way and soon each cell will have a toilet and wash hand basin. There is central heating, a new kitchen was commissioned in 1993 and a portion of the old jail has been renovated to provide excellent visiting facilities.

The new kitchen building.

The new kitchen and internal corridors enable meals to be delivered to the wings without having to cross the open yards in all weathers. Cold food was, until recently, a persistent and valid complaint. However, times have since changed. Here is a typical day's menu taken at random:

Breakfast: Choice of: Cornflakes. Weetabix. Rice Krispies. Warm Roll. Toast. Tea. Margarine. Marmalade.
Saturday and Sunday only: Grilled bacon. Sausage. Egg – fried or scrambled. Fried bread. Baked beans or tomato. Tea. Margarine. Bread.
Porridge is served once a week.

Dinner: Choice of: Beef and tomato pancake. Fried liver and onions. Macaroni cheese. Pizza.
Potatoes. Parsley, Carrots.

Tea: Choice of: Breast of Lamb. Chicken portion. Pork and apple. Vegetable casserole. Croutons.
Mashed potatoes. Cabbage. Chocolate blancmange with coconut.

Supper: Chelsea bun. Tea.

Special menus are provided for vegans, vegetarians, Muslims, Jews, and the sick men in the prison hospital.

It's not luxury and the men eat alone in their cells, but the food is wholesome and keeps a man healthy. The Governor tastes the food and enters his approval in the daily Kitchen Journal.

A dozen women officers are among the 140 disciplinary staff who patrol the wings night and day. I am reliably informed they do a good job and a difficult one at times. They undergo precisely the same training as the men, including the arduous riot control course. Far from being the "Amazons" you might expect, they are very feminine with a great deal of human understanding. Another innovation where Dartmoor took the lead was in the appointment in 1989 of a female Assistant Chaplain, the Rev Isabel Russell, the first woman to hold such a position in a prison like "the Moor". A cheerful kindly lady of mature years, she is happy to be regarded as a "mother" figure as well as a spiritual one. Her duties take her to every part of the prison entirely unescorted. Anxious to be of practical help, she joined those who pioneered the Group Therapy sessions for sex offenders which has since been adopted by other prisons (Dartmoor was the first to try this approach to the problem).

In the old days only members of the Church of England, Roman Catholics and Jews were recognised. Today there are facilities for other Christian denominations,

Auxilliary Officer Sue Stevens whose father is a prison officer at Dartmoor.

Prison Officer Gerald Worth, a long serving officer from an old Princetown family.

such as Methodism, the Salvation Army, Society of Friends (Quakers) and other faiths including Buddhism and Islam.

Dartmoor is a Catagory "B" and "C" Training Prison. The lower catagory is "C" and this grade of prisoner is used for work outside the establishment proper, on the farm for example. More than 90% of inmates are employed and are paid a weekly sum ranging from £2.50 to a maximum of £8.15. This enables them to buy sweets, tobacco, and other small luxuries from the prison canteen. They are not permitted to have money so all transactions are "on the book". The work they do includes laundry, kitchen work, cleaning, and assisting the Maintenance Department. Training and education for selected men provides instruction in bricklaying, plastering, decorating, electronics, and some computer work. Most inmates have radios, some have caged birds, and various hobbies are allowed such as model making and painting. The work of the prison chaplaincy goes on every day and of course services are held each Sunday morning.

Inmates at work with modern sewing machines manufacturing boxer shorts. No more mailbags!

An inmate undergoing computer training in the Technology section of the Education Department.

"Down on the farm". Dartmoor Prison 1994.

Conclusion

"HER MAJESTY'S PRISON SERVICE SERVES THE PUBLIC BY KEEPING IN CUSTODY THOSE COMMITTED BY THE COURTS. OUR DUTY IS TO LOOK AFTER THEM WITH HUMANITY AND TO HELP THEM LIVE LAW ABIDING AND USEFUL LIVES IN CUSTODY AND AFTER RELEASE."

This is the maxim of the modern Prison Service and is prominently displayed at focal points throughout the prison. Today's philosophy regards inmates (no longer referred to as convicts) as having been sent to prison as a punishment — not to receive punishment. Prison officers are trained professionals now and many of them are ex-servicemen. The old-time convict would be amazed to see Dartmoor Prison with its relaxed atmosphere, inmates wearing their hair in a variety of styles — long and short — watching television during "association", and living in well-lit, warm accommodation. Yet, at the end of the day, the one thing all inmates past and present share is the desire above all else to be free. As one of them succinctly put it when asked how he liked his new modern cell: "I ain't too bothered mate — I just want to get out."

Will Dartmoor close? Not in the foreseeable future. Rumours of closure began as far back as 1891 when the small number of convicts held, coupled with the expense of running and maintaining the place, was thought to be unjustified. Nothing was done and nothing ever has been done towards positively closing it down. As long as Britain has a soaring crime rate and limited resources with which to build new prisons, Dartmoor will play its part in the safe custody of undesirable and often dangerous men.

Echoes from the Past

Confined to the "Black Hole" in 1813:

23 March   F. Bilat for striking a prisoner, who died shortly afterwards and taking away his
provisions by force.

6 April   F. Le Jeune for being one of the principal provision buyers in the prison, and
for writing bloodthirsty and threatening letters.

(From a book by Basil Thomson, former Governor)

In the 1870s a man endured 50 days out of three months on bread and water, being continuously reported for bad behaviour. (The system allowed three days "restricted diet" then one day on normal rations, before another three days restricted diet, and so on.)
(From an account of convict life at Dartmoor by a former prisoner)

In 1854 a convict appealed against a ten year sentence of transportation (to be served at Dartmoor) for setting fire to a house. *(From the Governor's Journal 1854)*

Recommended increases in Rates of Pay 23 March 1853:

M.Lineham, Principle Warder   (£66.10s. per year)   by £1.10s.
J.Henderson, Warder   (£56.5s. per year)   by £1.5s.
S.Head, Baker   (£58.15s. per year)   by £1.5s.
D.Mackenzie, Farm Bailiff   (£100 per year)   by £5.

(From the Governor's Journal 1853)

Dartmoor – a "dumping ground"?

Joseph Crove from Pentonville moved to Dartmoor. Conduct stated to be "thoroughly bad" having been punished 15 times and removed from *Warrior* hulk for violent and outrageous conduct for which corporal punishment and extended sentence had been awarded. *(From the Governor's Journal 1854)*

Examples of 19th century prison slang:

QUOD .....Prison.   CHOKEY ..3 days bread and water.   LAGGED ...Arrested.
LAGGING ..Period of sentence.   BURST ..Burglary. "Doing a burst".
PLANTING THE SWAG ..Hiding proceeds of robbery.   HOOKS ......Pickpockets.
COCKS ....Londoners.   GOWKS ....Countrymen.
TAKING IN THE CROAKER ....Fooling the prison doctor – malingering.
HER MAJESTY'S BAD BARGAINS ..Soldier prisoners.
SNOUT ..Tobacco. (Still used today).

(From an account of prison life by Michael Davitt, former Dartmoor prisoner)